Humane options for dealing with a deceased horse's remains

Respectful and responsible options for grieving horse owners

By

Linda Ann Nickerson

Gait
House
Press

Published in the United States by Gait House Press.

Printed in the United States of America.

2016

Cover and internal illustration/s:

Public domain photo

Humane options for dealing with a deceased horse's remains

Respectful and responsible options for grieving horse owners

By

Linda Ann Nickerson

Contents

Introduction

Any horse lover is heartbroken at the loss of a much-loved equine. Equestrians dream of scenic sunset rides, soft nuzzles, lovely trots across fabulous sand footing, or great gallops across lush green fields with their treasured mounts. Surely, equines can trot right into our hearts and stay forever.

However, as every long-time horse owner knows, humans often outlive their horses.

I've been there, and it's hard. When my first horse passed away, I had to face the dreaded decision of determining what to do with the remains of the marvelous mare. This heart-rending process is surely the most difficult season in horse ownership.

Four possible plans

When the worst happens, what is a grieving horse owner to do?

What are the options for dealing with the remains of a horse that has died?

In most areas, multiple possibilities may exist. Legal ramifications and costs may vary locally, so horse owners will need to confirm the details of each option with equine veterinarians and the appropriate government agencies. State and county laws vary, but most jurisdictions require animal carcasses to be removed within the first 24 to 48 hours after death.

Leaving a horse's remains in a stall to decompose or out in the elements for scavengers to pick are most certainly out of the question. Local or municipal landfills and composting facilities generally will not accept animal carcasses for disposal, either. Caring horse owners generally aim for more respectful solutions for laying their beloved equines to rest.

An experienced equine veterinarian may provide insights and recommendations for the removal and disposal of a deceased equine's remains. However, the vet is not to be expected to offer or participate in the actual process, even if he or she is present for the animal's death.

Essentially, a grieving horse owner may consider four basic choices. These include equine burial, equine cremation, equine rendering, and equine taxidermy.

Some of these procedures may sound less desirable than others, depending upon each horse owner's personal preferences and sensitivities. It's difficult even to consider the possibility, but it's essential and helpful to consider one's options before such a crisis occurs. If a horse is owned by multiple people, the advance decision is extra important.

Smart and caring horse owners also set aside funds ahead of time to cover their selected option. In fact, some horse retirement farms collect deposits when they accept senior boarding clients to allow for this eventual inevitability.

Note: Price ranges have been estimated at the time of publication, and they are subject to change. Amounts will vary with each provider and location.

1. **Equine burial**

A 750- to 1,500-pound horse likely cannot be buried in the backyard, as many family pets may be (in certain locales). However, some horse farms with sufficient acreage may be able to allot large enough areas for equine burial. In many cases, grieving horse owners must hire contractors or rent backhoes to accomplish this task. This can cost hundreds of dollars, depending upon local prices.

Governmental agencies, such as the state's Department of Natural Resources, spell out requirements for the burial of horses and other livestock. Buried pipes and utilities must have sufficient clearance, and animals must be covered with specific depths of soil. Often, the minimum horse burial depth is two to six feet. Also, the carcass may not be placed near a reservoir or waterway.

Many localities outlaw the burial of medically (as in chemically) euthanized animals.

In-ground burial of an equine may be a natural choice for a grieving horse owner, who may choose to install a stone or marker on the spot. However, if the horse owner should ever relocate, the horse's remains may not be excavated.

Some cemeteries may allow horses and other pets to be buried near their humans. This option is fairly rare, however, and it tends to be quite costly. Certain pet cemeteries may accept equines for burial as well.

2. Equine cremation

Cremation (or incineration) is a common practice for dealing with horse remains. Large animal veterinarians can usually facilitate this process or recommend professional animal cremation facilities to perform the service legally and efficiently.

The grieving horse owner must choose between private or collective cremation, and prices vary considerably (often ranging from hundreds to thousands of dollars). Private cremation is essential, though costly, if a single horse's ashes are to be returned for burial or keeping. Keepsake boxes, urns, and other commemorative containers may be purchased as well.

In addition, the equine owner must make arrangements for transporting the horse's body to the cremation facility. Special hauling professionals may be enlisted for this purpose.

3. Equine rendering

Horse rendering may sound particularly unappealing, but this is a commonly chosen option for dealing with equine remains as well and usually the least expensive choice. Essentially, an equine renderer will pick up equine carcasses and transport them to a facility for communal disposal. This process usually ranges in price, based on pickup charges, as well as mileage and local fees.

What will a renderer do with the horse's remains?

The renderer, also known as a knacker, may choose from multiple solutions for disposing of a horse's carcass. Commonly used options include biorendering, incineration, or feeding to carnivorous animals in zoos, farms, animal breeding operations, or wildlife facilities. In some locales, renderers may deliver equine remains for various sorts of repurposing.

The grieving horse owner who enlists a renderer may be wiser not to ask for such specifics.

Grieving horse owners who choose to call a renderer will likely want to step away from the stables when the truck arrives to load the horse. Renderers often make daily rounds, stopping at various farms to pick up multiple deceased animals. This process is not one any horse owner needs to see and remember.

In lots of boarding barns, fellow horsemen and horsewomen habitually distract one another when a renderer's truck pulls into the farm, so none will accidentally catch a glimpse of the cargo. It is not uncommon to pay the renderer, point him in the right direction, and then step inside or behind the barn until the truck departs.

4. Equine taxidermy

Historically, the bodies of a few famous horses have been preserved by taxidermy. Such subjects include:

- Australia's Phar Lap
- General Custer's Comanche
- Napoleon's Le Vizir
- Roy Rogers' Trigger
- Dale Evans' Buttermilk

These taxidermy horses (sometimes informally called stuffed horses) were placed in special display cased in various museums from Melbourne, Australia, to Paris, France.

Taxidermy of horses is costly, and this option has limited availability. The process itself is quite expensive. In addition, the horse owner must come up with a suitable space for storing or displaying the preserved horse. What's more, the taxidermy horse may require remounting after several years.

All of this adds up to make equine taxidermy a complex and costly endeavor, making it a tall order for the average horse owner.

Equine owners seldom select this option for dealing with the remains of their dearly departed horses. Many horse lovers may prefer to remember their horses in their full-life glory, rather than viewing their preserved and mounted bodies in taxidermy form.

Wild game may one thing, at least for hunting enthusiasts, but a beloved equine companion is another consideration altogether.

Additional options

In some locales, horse remains may be donated for veterinary research or education.

Horse mementoes may matter.

Many horse owners save souvenirs from their horses, perhaps gathering the items while their equines are still living.

- Horse hair, collected from the mane or tail, can be braided or woven into attractive and long-lasting jewelry, home decorating items, or horse tack. It may also be incorporated into pottery or other artwork.

- Horseshoes are frequently used to create door knockers, photo frames, wind chimes, or a host of meaningful mementoes.

- Horse halters may be used to make belts, plant hangers, and shelf anchors.

- Stall nameplates can become treasured decorations as well.

Some horse owners are fortunate enough to have the opportunity to breed a favorite mare or stallion during the horse's prime, so that they may have a young horse to carry on that equine's good traits. Certainly, the youngster cannot replace the parent's special spot in the horse lover's heart, but this offers some consolation as well.

Portraits are perhaps the most popular means of preserving memories of beloved horses. Nearly all equine lovers take and keep photos of and with their mounts. Plenty arrange for professional portrait shoots, particularly if they sense their horses may be entering their last days.

Advance planning is important.

Ideally, a horse owner will address the eventually inevitable possibility of the equine's demise (at least theoretically) long before such a tragedy occurs. This responsible step, often called pre-need planning, can make the process somewhat less stressful, when the sad event actually happens and proper decisions must be made for dealing in a personally acceptable manner with the treasured horse's remains.

After all, the horse who has carried its owner for such a long stretch deserves a suitable finale.

About the author

Linda Ann Nickerson is an avid equestrian, breeding and raising sport horses and competing in both English and Western riding.

An award-winning prolific writer and former public relations executive, holding a B.A. in English and an M.S. in Journalism, Linda Ann has worked as a promotional consultant and professional writer for more than three decades.

Linda Ann Nickerson writes news and feature columns for several well-known websites. Her published portfolio includes well over 5,000 web articles, as well as countless print pieces.

Additional books from Linda Ann Nickerson include:

- *25 Top Tips for Promoting Your Equestrian Event: Get the Herd Out*
- *Equine reveries: Do horse dreams pack deeper meanings?*
- *Horseplay Secrets: Learning in Rhyme from Equines Sublime*
- *Stealing Wonder: A Rhyming Race to Capture Grace*
- *What's in Santa's Sleigh This Christmas?*

and more.

www.ingramcontent.com/pod-product-compliance
Lightning Source LLC
Chambersburg PA
CBHW071328310526
45789CB00016B/1833